CW00957462

South Dorset Walks

Hugh Stoker

*with sketch maps and
photographs by the author*

*Mill House Publications
The Mill House, Seatown, Bridport, Dorset.
Tel: 01297 489756*

CONTENTS   Page

Introduction

MOST of the walks described in this booklet lie within a 12-miles radius of Weymouth and Dorchester. However, because it is such a fascinating area, both scenically and historically, I have also included a number of walks covering the entire Purbeck coast as far as Swanage.

The walks follow a circular route, beginning and ending where the motorist can conveniently park his car without causing an obstruction. As for the walks, their main objective is to seek out the beautiful and secluded places, where you are most likely to see the *real* Dorset and the wild creatures which live in it. This means that most of your walking will be along field paths, bridleways, cliff tracks, forest trails, prehistoric ridgeways, ancient drove roads and packhorse trails.

All the routes described are easily within the average walker's capabilities, but they *are* cross-country walks, and suitable footwear is essential. The best choice for all seasons is a pair of sturdy waterproofed walking boots with non-slip cleated soles - worn, of course, with thick woollen socks. Smooth-soled shoes should be avoided at all costs; they are slippery on grass, and can be dangerous on steep hill slopes and cliff paths.

Although sketch maps have been included in this book, I would like to stress that a fairly large-scale Ordnance Survey map will add considerably to the enjoyment and interest of your walks. Your best choice would be one of the 1:25000 scale maps detailed at the foot of the following page. These show public rights of way, field boundaries and a wealth of other information.

An inexpensive pocket compass will also prove very useful, particularly when exploring some of the more remote and seldom-used routes. The coastal walks are obviously well-trodden, and the paths clearly defined. On many inland walks, however, there may be no visible path when crossing grassy fields and meadows - just the stiles and gateways linking various sections of a right of way. On these "off-the-beaten-track" sections I have purposely made my directions much more explicit, and where necessary have included simple compass bearings for you to follow. You will find these particularly useful when your next objective - be it stile, footbridge or gateway - happens to be hidden on the far side of a hill, or behind some overhanging tree branches.

Finally, do please observe the Country Code when sampling these walks. Don't park your car where it will obstruct a narrow lane, or prevent tractors and trailers manoeuvering into a field gateway. If you have a dog, keep it under close control at all times. Keep it on a lead in sheep country, or near woodland game reserves.

Enjoy yourselves!

IMPORTANT NOTE:
ORDNANCE SURVEY MAPS

Since publication of previous editions of this book, the Ordnance Survey has introduced another type of 1:25000 map that is ideal for walkers. Known as the "Explorer" series, each sheet provides much wider coverage than the earlier "Pathfinder" maps. At the start of each walk described in this book we have therefore recommended the appropriate "Explorer" sheet, although readers who already possess the earlier "Pathfinder" maps can continue to use them.

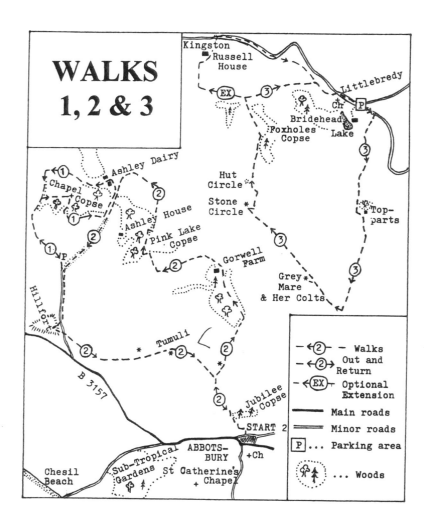

WALKS
1, 2 & 3

Kingston
Russell
House

Littlebredy

(EX) (3)

Ch
P

Bridehead
Foxholes Lake
Copse

Ashley Dairy

(1)

Chapel
Copse

(2)

Hut
Circle

Stone
Circle

Top-
parts

(1)

Ashley House

(1)

P

(2)

Pink Lake
Copse

(3)

(1)

(2)

Gorwell
Farm

(3)

Grey *
Mare
& Her Colts

Hillfort

Tumuli

(2)

*

(2)

*

(2)

(3)

B 3157

(2)

Jubilee
Copse

(2)

START 2

ABBOTS-
BURY

+Ch

Chesil
Beach

Sub-Tropical
Gardens

St Catherine's
+ Chapel

- ←(2)- — Walks
- ←(2)→ Out and
            Return
←(EX)— Optional
            Extension
─── Main roads
═══ Minor roads
P ... Parking area
🌳🌲 ... Woods

5

Walk No. 1

The Forgotten Chapel in a Wood

Abbotsbury Castle — Chapel Coppice — Ashley Farm —
Ashley Dairy — Abbotsbury Castle
Distances: (i) Approx 3¼ miles; (ii) Shortened version 2
miles.
O.S. Map: Explorer OL15 (1:25000); or 194 (1:50000).

TO reach the starting point for this short but very
pleasant walk you turn inland off the B 3157 coast road at
the "Ashley Chase" signpost, about 1 mile W of
Abbotsbury village. This takes you on to a narrow tarred
by-lane which climbs steeply around the flank of a
massive prehistoric hill fort known as Abbotsbury Castle.
After this the lane begins to descend again rather more
gently.

Soon you will see a notice board beside the lane
which reads: "PRIVATE — ASHLEY CHASE ONLY".
Stop the car just before reaching this notice and park on a
patch of grass which lies between the tarred lane and a
rough gravelly track which forks off in a N direction.

Walk along the gravel track for about ¾-mile until
you come to a dense wood bordering its right-hand (E)
side. This wood is called Chapel Coppice, and after walking along the edge of it for about 100 yards you'll come to
a stile, partly hidden by overhanging branches, which
gives access into the wood. A public footpath leads you
very pleasantly through the trees and alongside a small
stream bordered by steep ferny banks.

Then suddenly, as you glance up from picking your
way among the sprawling tree roots and bluebell clumps
you are confronted by the ruins of a small chapel. With a
supreme touch of drama, the woodland path enters the
arched doorway of the chapel, and immediately upon
passing through this entrance the first thing you notice is a
mossy stone altar surmounted by a weather-mellowed
shrine. In front of the altar are some recumbent memorial

stones to members of the Milne-Watson family, who used to own the Ashley Chase estate.

Although only the western gable-end wall of this ancient chapel remains standing, one nevertheless experiences a strange sensation of being "inside" a living place of worship. The one-time floor of the chapel is surrounded on its three open sides by walls of densely-growing trees; whilst overhead there is an over-arching "roof" of hazel branches and greenery.

Wander this way on a fine summer's evening, and maybe you'll be treated, as I was, to the sound of a thrush singing its vespers.

From the ruined chapel you will see paths wandering off through the undergrowth in several different directions, but your route on this walk keeps as close as possible to the authorised public right of way. Just outside the doorway arch of the chapel you follow a clearly defined path which heads through the trees in a SW direction, until it emerges from the wood after about 200 yards.

You now find yourself in open pastureland. Turn left and follow the edge of the wood, first in a S direction, and then turning E through a gated gap between the wood proper and a narrow out-jutting belt of trees. Soon you see some farm buildings ahead of you, with a farm road (classified as a public footpath) running alongside them.

Just beyond these buildings you come to an intersection of four private estate roads. Two alternatives are now open to you. For the shorter version of this walk, turn right and head uphill. This will take you directly back to your parked car.

However, the more interesting alternative is to turn left, and this is the route described in the remaining paragraphs.

(NOTE: Although the left- and right-hand roads are private, they are pedestrian rights of way. The road directly facing you is strictly private, however, and leads only to Ashley Chase House.)

After turning left (N) at the crossroads, and passing a picturesque thatched dwelling called "Shooting Box Cottage", your route descends steeply through a thick wood until, after crossing a small stream, it emerges into open country again. After another 200 yards or so you will see Ashley Dairy farm buildings nearby on your left. Turn left and walk past the first cottage; then turn left again (WSW) down a concrete-surfaced farm lane (bridleway) which crosses a stream and then climbs uphill alongside the N edge of Chapel Coppice.

After leaving the wood behind, the bridleway (there is no visible path) bears away NW through a gate, and then, on entering the next field, runs almost due W alongside a hedge. At the far end of this field it emerges through another gate on to a gravelly lane. This is, in fact, the lane you set out along at the start of your walk. Turn left along it, and after about 1 mile it will bring you back to your parked car.

Points of Interest

The Ruined Chapel, Ashley. Old records show that in medieval times the land at Ashley was held by Netley Abbey, a Cistercian monastery situated on the shores of Southampton Water. It is probable that monks from Netley began working a farm at Ashley at some uncertain date after the Abbey was founded in 1239, and one of their first tasks would have been to build a chapel in which to worship.

Walk No. 2

Exploring the Abbotsbury Hinterland

Abbotsbury — Gorwell Farm — Pink Lake Coppice —
Ashley Chase — Abbotsbury Castle — Wears Hill —
Abbotsbury (Free car park in Abbotsbury village)
Distance: Approx. 7 miles
O.S. Map: Explorer OL15 (1:25000); or 194 (1:50000).

ALTHOUGH thousands of people flock to
Abbotsbury every year to visit the famous Swannery and
Sub-Tropical Gardens, very few explore the high downs
and beautiful hidden valleys which lie just inland of this
picturesque and historic village.

Our walk today is designed to rectify this sad omis-
sion. It begins in Back Street — an aptly named lane
which branches off from Abbotsbury's main street
immediately opposite the post office-cum-general stores.
About 100 yards up Back Street you turn off to the left
along a narrow earth-surfaced bridleway which begins by
skirting the N edge of the village, and then starts climbing
the hillside towards a small wood called Jubilee Coppice.

Behind you, as the ground rises steeply, an interesting panoramic view of Abbotsbury begins to open up, and
you look down upon the time-mellowed cottages, church,
tithe barn and ravaged gateway of the vanished
Benedictine monastery as though they were the toy-sized
components of a model village. To complete the picture,
there is also the ancient chapel of St. Catherine, standing
alone and four-square to the winds on its green hilltop.

The bridleway continues to climb steadily alongside
the edge of Jubilee Coppice, but after leaving this belt of
woodland behind the track becomes less distinct, and its
course is marked only by a slight hollow in the grassy
hillside.

Before long, as you continue to climb the hillside, a
small but conspicuous open-sided hay barn comes into
view. Head towards this, and on the E side of it you will

find a gate through which the bridleway passes before bearing away to the NE up a steep slope where large greyish boulders protrude through the turf.

Soon, after passing a tumulus on your left, you arrive at a spot where your bridleway crosses a prehistoric ridge-way — now also classified as a bridleway. At this point there are three gates grouped together, and your route lies through the centre one. For the next 100 yards or so you head N, keeping a field fence close on your left. Then, on breasting the summit of the hill (height 634 ft) you will see a tract of woodland in the valley ahead.

The bridleway now bears away downhill to the NE, and then runs alongside the E edge of this wood until it brings you out on to a tarred farm lane. Turn left along this very pleasant lane, which for the next ¼-mile is bordered by woods.

Beyond these woods lies Gorwell Farm. Follow the bridleway past the farmhouse; then (just before reaching another nearby house over on your right) you turn off to the left (W) on to a minor track that is classified as a public footpath (no waymarks). Almost immediately you cross a tiny stream and enter a small stand of trees. Here the track divides. Take the left fork, which climbs a short slope and passes through a gateway into a grassy field. Continue W to meet the field boundary away on your right; then follow this hedge in a WSW direction.

After ½-mile you will come to a corner of the field, where a stile leads you into another grassy field immediately alongside a small plantation of conifers. From the nearest (E) end of this plantation, head N along-side the fence bordering the field until you come to the edge of a wood called, rather intriguingly, Pink Lake Coppice. In the corner of the field bordering the coppice is a stile which used to give access to a public footpath through the wood, but at the time of writing this long-established right of way has become completely lost under an impenetrable jungle of blackthorn and brambles.

Fortunately you can easily reach an alternative route by continuing W along the edge of the wood for about 100 yards until you come to a cart track that enters the trees in a N to NE direction.

Follow this track downhill, ignoring the first rather overgrown track which branches off to the right into the trees. After about ¼-mile, however, you will come to a second side-track branching off to the right. Turn down this, and after just a few yards it will lead you through a gateway into a grassy field. Turn right (E) on entering this field, and make towards a nearby hedgerow. Here you head NNE, keeping the hedge close on your right-hand side. (NOTE: At the time of writing, the 1:25000 O.S. map shows the public footpath following the other side of the hedge, but this route is no longer practical due to the disappearance of a stile).

On reaching the top end of the field you will come to a gateway. Here the right of way bears around towards the NW, and continues in this direction until it brings you out on to a hard-surfaced farm lane. Turn left (SW) along this lane, and head downhill towards the farm buildings of Ashley Dairy.

Continue straight on (SE) along this lane, passing the farm buildings about 100 yards on your right. This will take you up a steep hill through some thick woods.

On emerging from the trees you continue in a generally S — SW direction past thatched "Shooting Box Cottage", situated beside a cross-lanes. Head on S up a steepish hill until, after about a mile, the lane crosses the flank of an Iron Age hill fort known as Abbotsbury Castle. The entrance gap through the turf-covered ramparts lies close alongside the lane, and a brief diversion to explore this ancient stronghold of the local Durotriges tribe is well worthwhile. On a fine day the views from the S ramparts are truly magnificent.

On leaving Abbotsbury Castle you head SE across the tarred lane on to a grassy prehistoric trackway which follows the crest of the ridge overlooking the nearby coast. After ¼-mile the track passes the remains of a World War II look-out post, where a steel trap-door, set above the turf, gives access to a metal ladder which disappears mysteriously into the depths of the hillside. Peering down, one can see a tunnel heading inland from the bottom of the shaft. Several times, when passing this way, I have been tempted to clamber down to see where it leads to — but have always been deterred by the unpleasant thought that someone might happen along and bolt the trap-door while I was down below!

After about a mile of pleasant walking over springy turf, the track enters a field which has been put under the plough. The O.S. map shows the right of way heading directly across the field past a group of three ancient burial mounds. However, in summer, to avoid damaging growing crops, it may be necessary to skirt around the S edge of the field.

On reaching the far (SE) corner of the field you pass through a gap in the fence, and your route now begins to slant down the hillside in a SE direction. After passing a small overgrown quarry, you soon arrive back at the open-sided hay barn that you passed on the outward leg of your journey. From here you continue downhill past Jubilee Copse to Abbotsbury village.

Points of Interest

Abbotsbury Church. Just outside the porch of this beautiful, weather-worn old church you will see two ancient stone coffins, and propped up inside the porch there is a stone coffin lid, carved with the figure of an abbot holding a book and his pastoral staff. They almost certainly date back to the days of the great Benedictine abbey which was founded here during the reign of King Canute — and destroyed some 500 years later when Henry VIII ordered the dissolution of the monasteries.

The church contains many interesting links with Abbotsbury's eventful past, but possibly the most dramatic are two bullet holes in the wooden pulpit. These are relics of the Civil War, when fighting took place in the church as a preliminary to the storming of nearby Abbotsbury House, which was held for the King by Sir John Strangways.

The small group of Royalists inside the church, totalling 13 men, were soon overpowered and taken prisoner, but the siege of the manor house, built on the site of the old abbey, proved a tougher proposition.

Eventually, after six hours of bitter fighting, the house was set ablaze with burning furze faggots, and its occupants were forced to surrender. Whereupon a number of victorious besiegers dashed into the blazing building to plunder. While they were inside, the fire reached the Royalist gunpowder store, and all the would-be looters were blown up along with the house.

St. Catherine's Chapel. Built by the Abbotsbury monks around the 14th Century, this hilltop chapel commands a magnificent view of the surrounding coast and sea, and was a chantry for sailors. It contains many interesting architectural features, and is notable for the fact that it is built entirely of stone – no timber having been used in its construction. Situated about half a mile SW of the village, it is reached by a pleasant uphill walk that begins along a by-lane a few yards W of the post office.

Abbotsbury Swannery is situated on the shores of the Fleet – a shallow lagoon-like backwater behind the Chesil Beach. The swans were introduced here by the monks of the local monastery, who farmed them as a source of fresh meat during the winter months. Today the Swannery is run as a popular tourist attraction, and is normally open to the public from about late March to late October. Up-to-date information is available at local Tourist Information Centres, or direct from the Swannery – Tel: 01305 871858.

The Abbey Tithe Barn. This magnificent stone building, with its massive buttresses and thatched roof, was originally used to store the vast quantities of grain that passed through the ownership of the monastery. Today it contains the very popular Children's Farm. Leaflets giving full details are available at local Tourist Information Centres, or 'phone direct to the Swannery – see above.

The Pigeon House. This unusual building, with its dormer windows, stands a little way E of the tithe barn. In it the monks used to rear large numbers of pigeons as another source of fresh meat during the winter months.

The Sub-Tropical Gardens. These very beautiful gardens extend over approximately 20 acres. Originally established in the mid-1700's as a kitchen garden for Abbotsbury Castle (which no longer exists), it has since been developed into a spectacular sub-tropical garden filled with exotic trees and plants from all parts of the world. For details of opening times and admission fee (which also includes parking) telephone direct 01305 871130. It is also possible to purchase plants propagated from the many unusual and beautiful specimens growing in the garden. There is no admission fee to the nursery shop.

Walk No. 3
The Grey Mare and Her Colts

Littlebredy — Crow Hill — Grey Mare and Her Colts —
Kingston Russell Stone Circle — Foxholes Coppice —
Littlebredy
Distances: Approx. 5¾ miles; or with optional extension
via Kingston Russell House, 7 miles.
O.S. Map: Explorer OL15 (1:25000); or 194 (1:50000).

THE village of Littlebredy, where this walk begins,
is a tranquil place of scattered, time-mellowed cottages
nestling at the head of a secluded valley. There is also
Bridehead House, an impressive-looking mansion situated
beside a lake fed by crystal clear chalk springs. This lake is
the birthplace of the little River Bride, which makes its
meandering way to the sea at Burton Bradstock, some 9
miles distant.

Starting off from the public telephone box, which
stands conspicuously at the end of the village street, head
SE along the lane which skirts the grounds of Bridehead
House. After about 200 yards you will come to a gate leading into the village cricket ground. Here a signpost
indicates a bridleway which heads almost due S around
the boundary edge of the cricket field; then passes through
another gate and begins to climb a grassy, tree-dotted hillside beyond.

After gaining some height it is possible to look back
and obtain a fine bird's-eye view of Bridehead House,
with the southern end of the lake peeping out from behind
a dense mass of trees known as The Rookery.

Continuing uphill, the bridleway now runs along a
hollow worn in the turf by centuries of use. Before long,
at a height of 570 ft., the track begins to level off, and
ahead a small wood comes into view. This area is known
as Crow Hill but in recent years it seems to have become
the territory of a pair of buzzards. The last time I walked
this way, on a sunny day in high summer, the parent birds

were teaching their two youngsters the art of soaring flight, and the whole family were circling in the rising air currents, uttering their plaintive mewing cries.

The track skirts the W edge of this hill-top wood, and then passes through a gate marked with a blue arrow-head waymark. After passing a lonely farm building, your route settles down once more in a S direction. It is now easy level walking, with a fine view of Black Down and the Hardy Monument away to the left.

Before long you will probably be mystified to see a sign, in large red letters: "BEWARE OF LOW FLYING AIRCRAFT. KEEP TO THE BRIDLEWAYS".

If it happens to be a fine weekend, you may also be intrigued to see members of a model aircraft club putting their miniature radio-controlled machines through some spectacular aerobatics. The club members have mowed a small patch of this lonely hilltop and created a lawn-like mini-airfield. From its velvety green surface their models are flown off and landed with admirable skill.

A few hundred yards farther on the bridleway brings you to a gap in a hedge, through which can be glimpsed a tarred by-lane. Just before reaching this gap, however, you turn right (WNW) and continue along a grassy track which runs close alongside the hedge.

Before long you come to a signpost which reads: "KINGSTON RUSSELL STONE CIRCLE", and nearby there's a stile let into the hedge. Your route lies straight ahead, in the direction indicated by the signpost, but first of all I suggest you make a short diversion across the stile to visit "The Grey Mare and Her Colts" — this being the name given to a chambered megalithic tomb, formed of large flint-encrusted slabs of conglomerate rock.

The long barrow which originally covered the burial chamber has been eroded by the weather. The chamber itself was opened up early in the 19th Century, when many human bones and some pottery were found.

The view from this ancient burial site is superb, with a deep fertile valley immediately beneath the ridge, and rolling green hills stretching away westwards to the distance-hazed outline of Golden Cap.

Returning to the stile, you continue along the bridle-way in a NW direction, and soon come to a gap in the hedge where yet another signpost points the way to the Kingston Russell Stone Circle. In fact the ancient circle lies only 50 yards away in a cultivated field. When I visited this spot the stones were hidden in a colourful and aromatic crop of flowering vetches, but a pathway through the crop led to an uncultivated area of ground around the circle.

Erected about 1500 BC, during the Bronze Age, the Stone circle is 80ft in diameter, and was presumably used for religious purposes. The stones are now recumbent, but originally they probably stood upright. It is recorded that one stone was still standing in 1815.

The 1:25000 O.S. map shows a bridleway continuing NNW across the field from the stone circle, but there was no visible trace of this path when I visited the spot. There-fore, to avoid damaging the crop, I retraced my steps and walked around the edge of the field to the W fringe of a nearby wood called New Close Copse.

From here I headed NW for about 100 yards on to a spur of Tenants Hill. This brought me back on to the bridleway, which then continues N past the grassy remains of a prehistoric hut circle and enclosure before descending steeply towards the W edge of a dense wood called Foxholes Coppice.

About halfway along the edge of Foxholes Coppice the bridleway veers away in a NW direction towards a gap in a hedge. Passing through this gap, it enters another field which has gateways on its W and E sides. A public footpath runs between these two gates, and bearing away to the right you pass through the gate on the E side of the field. (See Note 1 below for details of an optional extension to this walk, taking the left-hand (W) path via Kingston Russell House).

After crossing a small stream, the footpath leads upwards in an ENE direction, offering a distant view of Kingston Russell House. After about ½-mile, during which you cross several fields and ford a shallow chalk stream, the path brings you out through a gateway on to the road leading into the W end of Littlebredy village. From here it is only a few minutes walk back to the parked car.

NOTE 1. Energetic walkers wishing to add another 1¼ miles to this route can turn W along the field path indicated on the sketch map. After crossing two fields this leads to a tarred lane. Turn right (N) along this lane to a sharp bend; then continue N along the private road (bridleway) leading to a charming old house called Watergate. Bear right here through a wicket gate and continue along the bridleway (now grass-grown and soggy in wet weather) which skirts the grounds of Kingston Russell House. This soon brings you to a tarred road, where you turn right and return to Littlebredy.

Points of Interest

Kingston Russell House. This stately house was once the home of the Russell family, which played such a notable role in English history over the centuries. The fortunes of this family really began in 1506, when a scholarly young squire called John Russell was urgently summoned from his home at nearby Berwick Farm. He was the only person in the district with a knowledge of Spanish, and he was needed to act as interpreter for Philip, Duke of Burgundy, heir to the throne of Castile.

The duke, with his wife Juana, had been sailing down-Channel to Spain to claim his kingdom when a severe storm forced them to take shelter in Weymouth. When King Henry the Seventh heard of their plight he invited the duke and his royal party to Court, and young John Russell accompanied them as interpreter. The king was well pleased with John Russell, and made him a gentleman of the privy chamber.

Three years later, when Henry the Eighth came to the throne, he quickly recognised John Russell's talents, and selected him for special military and diplomatic duties. One thing led to another — a knighthood, a rich marriage, a post as ambassador to the Pope, and many other high offices. When eventually Henry VIII died in 1547, Sir John Russell was one of his executors, and received the title of Earl of Bedford.

It is interesting to think that all this occurred because a small sailing vessel got caught in a storm near the notorious Portland Race. It's an ill wind that blows nobody any good!

Earthwork on Old Warren Hill. The early stages of this walk will take you within ½-mile of a rather unusual and apparently uncompleted hilltop earthwork known as "Old Warren", or "The Danes' Camp". There is written historical evidence, dating from about the 10th Century, which suggests that this turf-covered fortification may be the remains of one of King Alfred's burghs.

Walk No. 4

Around the Hardy Monument

Hardy Monument — Benecke Woods — Hardy Monument
Distance: Approx. 1½ miles.
O.S. Map: Explorer OL15 (1:25000); or 194 (1:50000)

VISIBLE for miles around, the massive monument to Sir Thomas Masterman Hardy dominates the heathery summit of Black Down, some 780 feet above sea level. This is not, of course, the Thomas Hardy of literary fame, but that other stalwart son of Dorset who was flag-captain to Lord Nelson on H.M.S. Victory at the Battle of Trafalgar.

The monument is a magnificent viewpoint, and on a fine day it is possible to look down upon a vast area of the

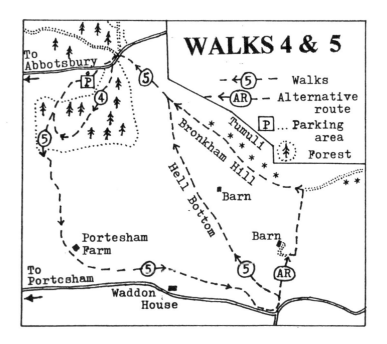

rolling green Dorset countryside. Far away to the south the shimmering, wave-flecked waters of Lyme Bay and Weymouth Bay are divided by the wedge-shaped bulk of the Portland peninsula, purple-hazed with distance.

Although thousands of sight-seeing motorists visit this National Trust beauty spot every year to admire the view and click their cameras, very few realise that it is also the centre of some magnificent walking country. In the short walk described here, and also in the medium-length Walk No. 5, we explore just a few of the footpaths and bridleways which thread their way through this most beautiful bit of Wessex.

After leaving your car in the large free parking area near the monument, return to the tarred road and head right (E) down a steep hill. After about 300 yards you turn right (SW) on to a path signposted: "Bridleway to Portesham 1½ miles". This path is bordered by heather, gorse, bracken and a pleasant mixture of coniferous and deciduous trees, and in due course it joins up with an unsurfaced forestry road. Turn right along this until you come to a fork in the track.

The left-hand fork head SW and leads to Portesham, but your route lies along the grassy right-hand fork. This soon begins to curve around to the NW, following the contours of the forested hillside. Before long, near a grove of thinned-out sycamores, your path joins up with another track. Turn right (N) and follow this new track up a steepish hill until it eventually leads you out of the forest just below the summit of Black Down. From here the Hardy Monument is clearly visible to guide you back to your parked car.

Although this is only a short walk, the terrain it covers is sheer magic — especially on a sunny day in late summer when the purple heather and golden gorse are both in full bloom.

Walk No. 5

From Black Down to Hell Bottom

Hardy Monument — Black Down Barn —Portesham Farm — Coryates Cross — Hell Bottom (or, alternatively Bronkham Hill) — Smitten Corner — Hardy Monument
Distances: Approx. 5¼ miles via Hell Bottom; or 5½ miles over Bronkham Hill.
O.S. Map: Explorer OL15 (1:25000); or 194 (1:50000).

AFTER parking the car near the Hardy Monument (for details see Walk No. 4), head roughly W across the heath for a little way until you encounter a track leading SW down the hillside towards a pine wood. Follow this track (it is classified as a bridleway) into the wood. From here you should continue SW, ignoring any side-paths, until eventually the track emerges from the trees again into open countryside.

On reaching the bottom of the valley you will come to a lone farm building called Black Down Barn. Here the track heads due S, passing between the barn and a large stone-walled cattle pen. After about 200 yards you come to a fork. Take the left-hand (SE) fork until you come to Portesham Farm. Continue past the farm buildings and through a gate which spans the track. A few yards beyond this gate, where the track bends sharply to the SW, you turn left through a gate into a grassy field. Head E across this field, following the contour of the hillside. This is a right of way, even though there is no visible footpath.

Aim for a gap in the wall at the far side of the field, and then across more fields, all the time heading roughly E and keeping fairly close to the crest of the ridge-shaped hill.

After a while you will catch a glimpse of Waddon House, half-hidden among trees at the foot of the hill on your right. The path then takes you past the ruins of an old lime kiln, with a disused quarry nearby.

A farm road curves up the hill past this old quarry. Turn left (N) and follow this track for just a few yards;

then turn right (E) and pass through a gate on to a grass track that follows the crest of the ridge. On nearing the far end of this ridge you should bear away to the SE, descending the side of the hill at an angle until you arrive at a gate leading out on to a tarred lane near a signposted T-junction.

Turn left (N) along the lane signposted: "Friar Waddon 1; Upwey 2¼". After climbing a short hill you come to a wayside fingerpost pointing to your left (W) which reads: "Bridleway to Hardy Monument 2 miles".

After turning on to this track you are immediately faced with a choice of routes, and both are equally attractive. You can either: (i) Veer left (WNW) to follow the bottom of a beautifully contoured valley called Hell Bottom; or (ii) continue N along a well-defined tractor track until it swings away sharply left to approach a lonely barn — whereupon you turn in the opposite direction (E) for just a few yards before turning N again and continuing up the side of Bronkham Hill, keeping a stone wall close to your left-hand side.

On reaching the crest of the hill you find yourself on a time-worn ridgeway bordered by bracken, heather and great thickets of golden-flowering gorse. Numerous ancient British burial mounds, half-hidden by the gorse clumps, flank the N side of the track; whilst away to S and W you are treated to a magnificent panoramic view that enables you to gaze upon the entire course of your day's walk.

Your route now lies through sheep country, so if you are accompanied by a dog you should put it on a lead. Eventually the two alternative routes join forces again — the Hell Bottom path gradually climbing up the valley to meet the Bronkham Hill track as it descends the NW end of the ridge.

In due course you arrive on a tarred by-road at a spot which bears the intriguing name of Smitten Corner. You now turn left up a steepish hill, and very soon arrive back at the Hardy Monument and your parked car.

Walk No. 6

Maiden Castle

Distance: Approx. 2¼ miles.
O.S. Map: Explorer OL15 (1:25000); or 194 (1:50000).

THE prehistoric hill fort known as Maiden Castle is situated only a mile or so from Dorchester's SW outskirts, and a walk around its massive turf-covered ramparts is not only an interesting experience, but will also treat you to some magnificent views of the surrounding countryside.

To reach the ancient stronghold by car, follow the Weymouth road to the outskirts of Dorchester, and then turn off at a junction clearly signposted: "Maiden Castle". Continue along this road until it ends at a free public car park.

Ahead of you a grassy track leads upwards to the W entrance of the hill fort. Make your way into the entrance until you have climbed to the level of the highest rampart. Here you will see a sign pointing to your left (NE) indicating the direction of the Romano-British temple. (See under *Points of Interest*). Follow this direction sign by climbing to the top of the rampart, and then continuing along its crest.

After just under ½-mile you will see the foundations of the temple a short distance away inside the ramparts. The remains are protected by a fence, but a stile and gate provide access to the site.

Having viewed the temple, return to the crest of the inner rampart. From here it is only a short distance to the E entrance of the hill fort, where in AD 43 a fierce battle was fought between the British inhabitants and a beseiging Roman army under Vespasian.

After completing the circuit of the ramparts you return to the parked car by descending through the W entrance.

Points of Interest

Maiden Castle. The original Celtic name of this prehistoric fortress was probably "Mai-Dun", which has been interpreted tentatively by some as meaning "The Hill of Strength". Excavations have revealed that a neolithic (late Stone Age) village, surrounded by a single ditch and rampart, was situated at the E end of the hilltop about 4,000-5,000 years ago. Later on, but still during the neolithic period, a huge bank barrow measuring 1740 ft in length and 60 ft wide was built for some obscure reason along most of the length of the hilltop. Little now remains of this mound, but excavations near its E end uncovered a mutilated human skeleton which had apparently been buried beneath the mound during its construction.

The hill fort as we see it today, with its massive triple ditched ramparts encircling the entire perimeter of the hilltop, was constructed during the Iron Age. Obviously, with the primitive tools of that period such a formidable task occupied the lifetimes of many generations, and it was not until about 200-100 BC that the fortifications, after being repeatedly modified and enlarged, eventually began to near completion.

The final touches to the defences included a stone parapet around the inner rampart. This has now vanished, although its foundations still provide a firm walking surface around the crest of the rampart. The entrances, too, were reinforced with massive stone revetments, and excavated remains of these can be seen near the E entrance.

The main weapon used by the inhabitants of Mai-Dun was the sling, which in the hands of an expert is capable of hurling a stone with deadly force and accuracy. The hill fort's tiered ramparts were therefore designed to give maximum advantage to a defending force using this weapon. This advantage stemmed from the fact that a sling stone hurled downhill by a defender had considerably greater range and hitting power than a stone hurled upwards by an attacker.

This simple but very effective defensive strategy worked well enough until the Romans invaded Britain. Their deadly machine arrows out-ranged the sling stones of the native Britons, even when attacking uphill.

As the Roman army advanced into the territory of the Durotriges tribe, one fortified hilltop township after another fell to the invaders. Finally came the siege of the tribal capital of Mai-Dun, and after a bitter battle the Romans broke through its eastern entrance. Many of the defenders, including women and children, were put to the sword. Excavations in 1937 revealed their skeletons, bearing signs of sword and arrow wounds, buried hurriedly just outside the E entrance. One skeleton still had the head of a Roman machine arrow embedded in its spine.

The hilltop town continued to be occupied by the survivors for another 20 years or so — after which the inhabitants moved down into the new Roman town of Durnovaria (Dorchester).

The Roman Temple was built about 300 years after the Roman invasion by the local Romano–British inhabitants, who probably still nurtured a sentimental attachment for the hilltop dwelling place of their ancestors. Archaeological finds on the site included a small bronze Celtic statuette of a deified bull, and a bronze plaque of Minerva — the goddess of wisdom and good counsel. Other finds included a Roman brooch, coins and a gold ring.

Dorchester Museum contains many fascinating objects found in this hill fort, and a visit will add considerably to the enjoyment and appreciation of this walk.

Walk No. 7

Over Hampton Hill to Frampton Park

Hampton Lodge — Hampton Hill — Frampton —
Frampton Park — Hampton Lodge
Distances: Approx. 6¾ miles; or shortened route, 5 miles.
O.S. Map: Explorer OL15 (1:25000); or 194 (1:50000).

THIS very pleasant walk takes one through varied
scenery, ranging from rolling chalk downlands to tranquil
water meadows and parklands beside the River Frome. To
reach the starting point by car, take the A35 Dorchester to
Winterborne Abbas road, but turn off on to the old
Roman road about ¾-mile NE of Winterborne Abbas.

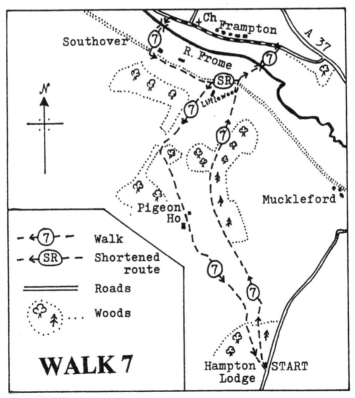

After a few hundred yards you will come to a cross-roads. Turn right here along a by-road signposted "Muckleford", and after ¾-mile you'll see Hampton Lodge on your left. DO NOT drive into the lodge entrance (it is a private road); instead, park on the grass verge beside the Council road.

There is a pedestrian right-of-way along the private drive leading past the lodge, and immediately after passing this cottage you take a right-hand fork which is classified as a bridleway. This will lead you through a small patch of woodland before emerging on to open grassy downland.

The track now climbs gently upwards, passing through several gates. It then skirts the edge of another wood before breasting the summit of Hampton Hill. You have now reached the highest point on your walk (about 500 ft above sea level), and ahead some grand views begin to open up across the Frome valley towards the rolling chalk downs beyond.

The path now begins to tilt downhill, and soon enters a plantation of beech and sycamore which, in spring and early summer, is alive with birdsong. Just before reaching the far side of this wood you take a right-hand fork in the track. This soon leads you out of the trees on to a wide expanse of grassland. All visible trace of the bridleway disappears after leaving the wood, but if you head across the grass in a NNE direction you will eventually come to a gate which leads out on to an estate road.

Continue straight on (NNE) down this road towards a second intersecting estate road (classified as a bridle-way) barely 100 yards further on. Here you turn right (NE), and very soon come to a graceful stone bridge with lichen-dappled balustrades. This takes you across the swift-flowing River Frome, and then up past Peacock Lodge on to the Dorchester-Maiden Newton road, where you turn left into nearby Frampton village. Incidentally, Peacock Lodge derives its name from the peacocks which, in the hey-day of the Frampton estate, used to wander around this gate-keeper's cottage and the adjoining wood called Peacock Plantation.

The village of Frampton straggles picturesquely along the N side of its main street, whilst the opposite side of the road is bordered by a belt of noble trees. The church contains a number of unusual features, and is well worth a visit. (See under *Points of Interest*).

After leaving the church, continue W along the village street for about 250 yards; then turn left down a lane signposted: "Southover". After crossing the Frome again, you turn left (SE) at a fingerpost indicating a bridleway.

This leads you past The Court, a modern and more compact replacement for the original Frampton Court — a stately house that was demolished in 1932 after the estate had been sold to pay death duties. All that now remains of the old mansion is the massive stable block and laundry, which you pass on your left. These have now been converted into dwellings.

Soon after this you approach the old Littlewood farm buildings. Just before reaching these you turn right (S) along a track that is classified as a pedestrian right of way. Follow this in a SW direction for ½-mile until you come to a bungalow called "Medlands".

Almost directly opposite this bungalow you will see a grassy track forking off to your left. It begins by heading SW, but soon curves around and heads SE. Eventually, after skirting some more farm buildings, it joins an estate road and passes a beautiful house surrounded by stately chestnut trees. It bears the intriguing name of "The Pigeon House".

Still heading SE, your route leads you through pleasant tree-dotted parkland grazed by cattle; then, after tunnelling through a small wood, brings you back to Hampton Lodge and your parked car.

NOTE: Anyone lacking in time or energy can, if they wish, shorten this circular walk to about 5 miles by heading direct from the point indicated on the sketch map to the footpath turn-off just E of Littlewood farm buildings.

Points of Interest

Frampton Village and Church. For centuries this village and neighbouring lands belonged to the Benedictine Abbey of St. Stephen, of Caen, in Normandy, having been given away by William the Conqueror. Some monks from Caen built a priory just across the River Frome, in what later became Frampton Park. Ancient records show that in 1293 it was the wealthiest monastic foundation in Dorset.

Frampton church contains many interesting features, and not least of these is the stone pulpit — one of the best of its kind in Dorset. Within the church you will also see numerous memorials to the Browne family, who bought Frampton during the days of Elizabeth I, and remained Lords of the Manor for many centuries.

Roman aqueduct. Traces of a Roman aqueduct can still be seen here and there along the S side of the Frome valley. It appears to have been a simple open leat cut in the chalk, but skilfully engineered to make best use of the natural contours of the land. Its probable purpose was to tap the waters of the River Frome to supply the ornamental fountains and public baths of Roman Dorchester — then known as "Durnovaria".

Walk No. 8

Thorncombe Wood Nature Trail

Thorncombe Wood — Black Heath — Thorncombe
Wood
Distance: **Approx. 1½ miles.**
O.S. Map: Explorer OL15 (1:25000); or 194 (1:50000).

SITUATED only a few hundred yards from Hardy's
birthplace cottage in Higher Bockhampton, and adjoining
a free car park, the 46 acres of mainly deciduous woodland
known as Thorncombe Wood is managed by Dorset
County Council as a natural wildlife sanctuary. The
nature reserve also includes 20 acres of adjoining open
heathland (Black Heath) which provides a stark contrast
to the secluded woodland scenery and ecology.

A very interesting nature trail meanders through the
wood and across the heath, and this is open to the public

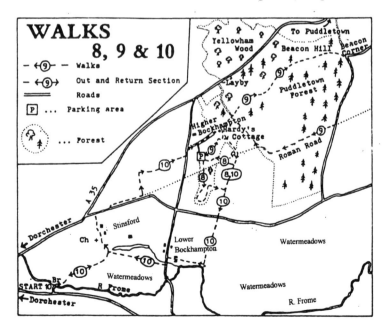

free of charge. The only thing asked in return is that visitors keep to the waymarked paths to avoid undue disturbance to wildlife, and that every care be taken against starting fires. Wild flowers, needless to say, should not be picked, but left for others to enjoy.

Incidentally, on your left as you enter the car park, you will see some excellent display panels showing the main points of interest to be found along the nature trail, together with colour illustrations of the local flora and fauna.

NOTE: To reach this car park from Dorchester, follow the directions given in the introductory paragraph to Walk No. 9. Keen walkers, eager to explore the area at greater length, can conveniently combine this short nature trail with Walk No. 9, as the same car park is the starting point for both routes.

The ruined gable end of St. Luke's Chapel provides a dramatic frame for the lonely woodland altar shrine.
(Walk 1).

A closer view of the altar shrine.

The Western end of 18 miles long Chesil Beach. Golden Cap can be seen in the distance.

The small town of Cerne Abbas is steeped in history. One of its most attractive features is this ancient dwelling, situated opposite the church. (Walk 11)

Walk No. 9

Hardy's Cottage and Puddletown Forest

Thorncombe Wood car park - Hardy's Cottage - Puddletown Forest - Beacon Corner - Roman Road - Hardy's Cottage - Thorncombe Wood car park.

Distance: Approx. 5 miles.

O.S. Map: Explorer OL15 (1:25000); or 194 (1:50000).

NOTE: Puddletown Forest is criss-crossed with a veritable maze of tracks and paths, and at the time of writing hardly any are waymarked or signposted. For this reason we recommend that you carry a compass.

To reach the starting point for this walk from Dorchester, drive E out of the town to the by-pass roundabout, where you turn off on to a minor road and follow signs to Higher Bockhampton and Hardy's Cottage. Turn right down a gravel lane to a free car park on the edge of Thorncombe Wood.

Enter Thorncombe Wood along the path leading to Hardy's cottage. (For viewing times see under **Points of Interest**).

When the famous novelist was a boy, in the mid-1800's, the cottage was a favourite meeting place for the local Stinsford church choir, of which both Hardy's father and grandfather were leading members. In those days the village choir had its own small orchestra of local musicians. Some of them even played on home-made instruments like the old Dorset humstrum - a primitive and none-too-melodious member of the fiddle tribe.

We can imagine young Thomas Hardy sitting in the chimney corner of the cottage kitchen, listening to the singing and playing, and to the backchat and tall stories of his elders. Doubtless these activities became noisier as throats were lubricated with the inevitable home-made cider, and there's no doubt that many of these village characters and their yarns found their way into Hardy's novels and poems.

To continue your walk, exit the cottage garden by a side gate into a lane. Here you turn right and continue along a waymarked bridleway which heads NE into Puddletown Forest.

After about ¼-mile you come to a clearing where six tracks converge. To avoid confusion later on, pause a moment to memorise carefully which track you have just travelled, because you will be returning to this spot (by a different track) towards the end of your circular walk.

Continue straight across this intersection, taking the track which heads on into the forest in a roughly NE direction. During the next mile or so you will encounter several more side-tracks leading off to left and right, but provided you keep as close as possible to your NE heading you cannot go wrong. In due course the trail begins to descend steadily, and eventually brings you out on to a tarred road at Beacon Corner.

Here you turn right and follow this little-used by-road which, for much of the way, is hedged on both sides with rhododendrons. Continue on past the first broad track on your right leading back into the forest (it is guarded by a green barrier). After about ½-mile you come to a second track leading into the forest. Take the broad main track which heads straight into the forest, ignoring a waymarked bridleway which veers off to the right just inside the entry barrier.

After only 100 yards you turn off to the left along a side track which soon heads off through the pines in a straight line towards the SW. It is, in fact, the Roman road that once led to nearby Durnovaria (Dorchester).

Twice within the next half-mile the old road is

crossed by broad forestry tracks, but your route lies straight on in the wake of the ghostly legions. Soon, at the foot of a steep rise you come to a fork. Take the left fork, and as it curves and climbs around the hillside the old road becomes narrower, hemmed in by encroaching trees.

Before long the Roman road joins a footpath. Turn right and continue straight on (NNW) along this path, which soon brings you to the intersection of six tracks mentioned earlier in these directions. Take the track you memorised on your outward journey (the second on your left) and retrace your steps to Hardy's Cottage and the Thorncombe Wood car park.

Points of Interest

Hardy's Cottage. At the time of writing the exterior can be viewed free 1 April to 1 November from 11am to 5pm, or dusk if earlier - Fridays and Saturdays excepted, but open Good Friday. To view interior 'phone 01305 262366 for up-to-date admission fee and details

The Roman Road. Prior to recent afforestation this stretch of the old road crossed a tract of open heathland - a last remnant of the vast "Egdon Heath" of the Hardy novels. Thomas Hardy must have walked this way before penning the following lines from his poem, *The Roman Road:* "The Roman Road runs straight and bare

As the pale parting line in hair,
Across the heath. And thoughtful men
Contrast its days of Now and Then,
And delve and measure and compare.
Visioning on the vacant air
Helmed legionaries, who proudly rear
The Eagle, as they pace again
The Roman Road."

Walk No. 10
By Meadows, Woodland and Heath

Dorchester — Stinsford — Higher Bockhampton — Hardy's Cottage — Thorncombe Wood — Black Heath — Lower Bockhampton — Stinsford — Dorchester.

Distance: Approx. 6½ miles when starting and ending near the St. George's Road allotments, Dorchester; or 8 miles from the Town Centre.
O.S. Map: Explorer OL15 (1:25000); or 194 (1:50000).

THIS very pleasant field path route linking Dorchester and the tiny hamlets of Stinsford and Higher Bockhampton must have been trodden by Thomas Hardy on countless occasions in his younger days when visiting the bustling market town from his birthplace cottage. (See Walk No. 9, Points of Interest).

Although this circular walk can start and end at several places along its route (Higher Bockhampton, Stinsford or Lower Bockhampton), for convenience we will begin these directions in St. George's Road, on the E outskirts of Dorchester. About a ¼-mile along this road a cart track leads off to the N past some allotment gardens. From here you can cross the River Frome by a small bridge, and then follow a public footpath NE across a broad expanse of watermeadows. After crossing a small footbridge, your route joins up with another footpath on the S outskirts of Stinsford. Turn left (W) on to this new path: then (after only a few yards) turn right (NNW) on to a path leading to nearby Stinsford Church. In this churchyard, in 1928, the heart of Thomas Hardy was laid to rest alongside his first wife. His ashes lie in Poet's Corner, Westminster Abbey.

From Stinsford Church you make your way to the N outskirts of the tiny village, where you turn right (ENE) along a tarred by-lane. After about 300 yards you will see a fingerpost in the hedge on your left which reads: "Footpath to Hardy's Birthplace". Take this path, which continues ENE along the grass-covered foundations of a Roman road. After about 500 yards, turn left (NNW) along a bridleway track that runs across some fields. At the far end of the first field you turn right (E) off the bridleway on to a rather indistinct footpath, keeping the field fence close on your *left*. Soon you pass through a waymarked gate on your left and head NE along the edge of another field towards a conspicuous nearby farm building. This brings you on to an unsurfaced lane. Head ENE down this lane, and turn left when you come to a tarred road; then, after only a few yards, turn right along a lane signposted: "Hardy's Cottage".

From the rear (N Side) of Hardy's Cottage, head SSE along a well-trodden woodland path for about 50 yards. As you do so, keep a sharp look-out for a tree on your left with a yellow arrow painted on it, pointing the way on to a lesser-used footpath.

This path will lead you through the woods in a SSE direction. Soon, after crossing a stile, you emerge on to a tract of heathland known as Black Heath. Continue SSE, keeping the edge of the forest on your left. Before long you will come to a small pond, where deer, badgers, foxes and many other wild creatures come to drink at night. Their spoor can often be seen in the muddy edges of the pond. Notice, also, the "badger gate" set in the fence bordering the left-hand side of the path. Badgers are creatures of habit, and insist on using the same paths that their ancestors have used over the centuries. Without that flap-gate, they would simply force a way through the fence!

Continue SSW, passing the pond on your right. This stretch of path, we are told, rejoices in the name of "Snail's Creep", and was once used by smugglers when transporting their illicit kegs to inland disposal points.

About 250 yards after leaving the pond you will come to a bend in the path. Here, instead of following the well-trodden woodland path, you continue SSW, passing through a nearby gate into an open field where you follow the course of a hedge on your right.

This right-of-way leads you through another gate on to a farm road, which in turn brings you out on to a tarred by-road.

Continue SSW straight across this road on to another track signposted to Bhompston Farm. On reaching the farm, turn right (W) along a grassy path which takes you over a waymarked stile; then across a meadow to a gate leading into the farmyard of Kingston Dairy House. The public right-of-way leaves the farmyard by another gate on the W side. From here a lane leads you into the "main street" of Lower Bockhampton. Turn left (S) and follow this road for 100 yards. Then, after crossing a stream, turn right along a very pleasant causeway footpath which leads you between the park-like grounds of Kingston Maurward House and the watermeadows bordering the River Frome.

After ½-mile this path brings you back to the S outskirts of Stinsford, and from here you return to Dorchester across the watermeadows, following the path used on the opening stages of your walk.

Points of Interest

Stinsford Church. Referred to as "Mellstock Church" in Hardy's novel, "Under the Greenwood Tree", this 13th century church is well worth a visit. Hardy's grandfather, father and uncle were leading members of the church choir for over forty years, and the characters and events associated with the "Mellstock Quire" and its musicians frequently found their way into his writings. In his poem, "The Dead Quire", written after several older members of the Stinsford choir had passed on, Hardy conjures up a spine-tingling Christmastide scene, in which a group of phantom singers wander along the riverside path leading to the church, and then vanish into the graveyard.

It was in this same graveyard, incidentally, that a Norman font was unearthed some years ago, broken into seven pieces. Carved out of Purbeck marble, it was clearly a relic of considerable historic interest, and was skilfully reconstructed. Today it stands once more inside the church, and within the font you will also see an ancient stone bowl, believed to be a stoup for holy water, which was found nearby.

Another interesting relic, situated in the south wall of the chancel, is a 13th century piscina which was found buried alongside the church.

Walk No. 11
The Cerne Giant . . . and beyond
Cerne Abbas - Giant Hill - Foxhills - Black Hill - Cerne Abbas

Distance: Approx. 5 miles.

O.S. Map: Explorer 117 (1:25000); or 194 (1:50000).

TO reach the starting point for this walk you drive along the A352 Dorchester-Sherborne road to the outskirts of Cerne Abbas, where you can either park your car on the layby overlooking the Cerne Giant, or preferably follow the direction signs down a side road to a parking space in a nearby picnic area.

From the picnic area you cross a nearby stone bridge over the River Cerne, and shortly afterwards bear left and take the footpath which climbs the turfy hillside towards the Giant. (See under *Points of Interest).*

The hill figure has been protected from erosion by a perimeter fence erected by the National Trust. Follow this fence around to its upper (NW) corner, where you will be able to view the associated earthwork known as the Trendle.

From here you continue uphill in a generally NE-NNE direction until you encounter a turfy contour track which skirts arount the 700ft crest of the hill. The views from this vantage point are magnificent. The steep hillside curves around to form a vast natural amphitheatre and down below a broad expanse of fertile arable land, called Yelcombe Bottom, occupies the space between the encircling hills. Away to the SE, at the mouth of the amphitheatre, lies the village of Cerne Abbas - "curled up like a dormouse in a sunny corner" as one early guidebook writer so aptly described it.

It will save a lot of tedious directions if I tell you that

Fishermen launching their boats off the rock ledges of Portland Bill. (Walk 13)

Abbotsbury village with its thatched abbey tithe barn in the foreground. The prehistoric ridgeway explored on Walk 2 lies along the distant hilltop skyline.

The abbey gatehouse at Cerne Abbas, notable for its magnificent oriel window. (Walk 11)

Bluebell time in Dorset. Wildflowers add a touch of magic to many woodland footpaths.

for the next mile or so your route follows the rim of this amphitheatre. Eventually, after circling around its NE end, you come to a minor road running downhill towards Cerne Abbas. Follow this road for ¼-mile until you come to the entrance gate of a house called "Foxhills". On the opposite side of the road you'll see a field gate. Pass through this and head uphill in a SSE direction. Although this is a right of way there is no visible path, but you will not go far wrong if you aim for the top end of the wood which you will soon see ahead of you.

After passing the wood head S alongside a hedge; then make for a gateway which leads out on to a tarred lane. Turn right down this lane, alongside a hanging wood on your right, and before long it will bring you into Cerne Abbas.

On reaching the village make your way to St Mary's Church, which contains many interesting features. Notice also the row of overhung Tudor dwellings just across the road from the church entrance. On one of them the exterior plaster has been removed to reveal the ancient timbers and some interesting carving.

After leaving the church continue up the lane leading to the beautiful gabled Abbey House, built from the stones of Cerne Abbey after it was demolished. Originally a farmhouse, it is said that an uncle of George Washington once lived there.

About midway between the church and Abbey House a footpath leads off to the left (W). Follow this and turn right on reaching the little River Cerne. The path will then lead you very pleasantly alongside the stream to the stone bridge that you crossed at the outset of your walk.

Points of Interest

The Cerne Giant. This figure of a nude man has been

cut into the grassy hillside, and outlined with the natural white chalk subsoil. The giant is 180ft tall, and the club he wields in his right hand is 120ft long. Experts consider him to be of Romano-British origin, and about 1,300-1,500 years old. Long regarded as a symbol of fertility, there is some evidence that his traditional local name was Helis or Helith.

The Trendle is a low grassy mound and enclosure just above the Giant. Its origin is uncertain, but it is said to have been used for maypole dancing.

Cerne Abbey. Of this once great Benedictine abbey, founded in 987, little now remains except the stone gatehouse, with its decorated two-storied oriel window, and the 14th century building that the monks reserved for visiting pilgrims or guests. This guest house stood outside the walls of the monastery to reduce the risk of plague. The abbey ruins are situated near Abbey House, and may be visited on payment of a small admission fee which (at the time of writing) goes to charities.

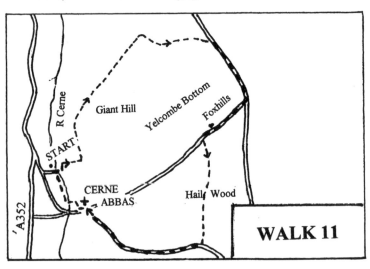

Walk No. 12

The Land of Far Horizons

Godmanstone — Reynard's Copse — Pond Bottom —
Huish Farm — Sydling St. Nicholas — Large Bar Hill —
Godmanstone
Distance: Approx. 8½ miles
O.S. Map: Explorer 117 (1:25000); or 194 (1:50000).

ONLY a few miles north of Dorchester there is a
large tract of rolling chalk downland that is completely
devoid of human habitation. Roughly triangular in shape,
and bounded by the villages of Charminster, Cerne Abbas
and Sydling St. Nicholas, this beautiful area of lonely hills
and distant horizons is criss-crossed by numerous public
footpaths and bridleways.

Our walk today begins in Godmanstone — a pleasant
little village on the A 352 about 2 miles S of Cerne Abbas.
The village is, perhaps, most notable for its toy-sized pub,
"The Smith's Arms". It is so tiny that even a half-grown

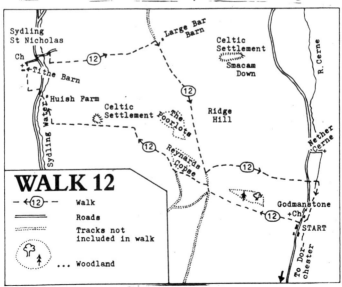

child could probably reach up and touch the eaves of its thatched roof with outstretched fingers. Outside the inn, tables and chairs stand invitingly beside a watercress-fringed trout stream that is the stripling River Cerne.

About 50 yards S of the "Smith's Arms", and on the opposite side of the road, a fingerpost indicates the start of a bridleway to Sydling St. Nicholas. You head WNW along this track, which for the next mile climbs steadily uphill beside arable fields which, in late summer, are usually glowing with the gold of ripening corn.

Eventually, on reaching the crest of the hill, you pass through a gate and find yourself on a prehistoric ridgeway of springy turf, which extends N and S as far as you can see. On the far side the land drops away steeply, treating you to a magnificent view of the rolling Dorset countryside.

As previously mentioned, all the local farms and cottages are concentrated in the valleys, leaving these hills completely deserted. This was not always the case. Long ago, before the arrival of the Romans, the Celtic farming folk established their fields and settlements on these uplands, and during the course of this walk you will see numerous traces of their long occupation — including, of course, the turf covered tracks they once trod thousands of years ago. Most of these ancient tracks have now been classified as bridleways and public footpaths.

A glance at your O.S. map will reveal that this spot, where you are now standing, is in fact the meeting place of five tracks. In the heyday of the Celts it must have been the prehistoric equivalent of Piccadilly Circus!

Anyway, having recovered your breath, it's time you pressed on with your walk. Turning right (N) along the ridgeway, you head towards a nearby fence, where you turn left (NW), keeping the fence on your right-hand side. The narrow strip of unploughed grass beside the fence soon leads on to a well-worn track, which descends around the rim of a huge, amphitheatre-shaped hollow in the hillside. The prevailing updraughts formed by this natural windscoop make this a favourite hunting area for sail-gliding buzzards, and the air hereabouts is usually filled with the sound of their plaintive mewing cries.

At the bottom of this hillside the track curves away to the right (NNW) along a grassy valley called Pond Bottom. Nearby, on your right, you'll see a small enclosure of scrubby trees called Reynard's Copse. When I walked this way in late summer I found the lower end of the copse festooned with several of those large battery-operated flashing hazard warning lanterns that one normally associates with major road works.

Investigating closer, I discovered that these devices had been put there to protect some young pheasants from predators. Obviously Reynard still goes a-hunting in this copse after nightfall!

The track now passes through a gate, and heads NW past a small hay barn before running alongside a wire fence. Keep this fence on your left, and continue to follow it when, in due course, it makes a sudden left-hand turn towards the W. A well used track now leads upwards on to the summit of Shearplace Hill, where numerous grassy hollows and mounds mark the site of an ancient Celtic settlement.

Still heading due W, you now descend steeply into the next valley. At the bottom of the hill the track veers NNW, and passes picturesque Huish farmhouse — a beautiful old dwelling flanked by a stately copper beech tree and a quietly flowing chalk stream.

A few yards farther on you emerge on to a tarred lane leading to nearby Sydling St. Nicholas. Turn right along this road; then, after about 50 yards, turn left on to a pleasant green lane flanked by high over-arching hedgerows.

After a few hundred yards this green lane joins a grassy drove road. Here you turn right (due N), and very soon come to the farmyard of Court Farm, where stands a fine old tithe barn.

Although corrugated iron has now replaced its original roof of thatch, the barn still possesses its oak roof timbers, and it is well worth pausing for a minute to study the impressive assembly of tie and collar-beam trusses, and curved braces. On one of these beams there is carved, so it is said, the inscription: "UW 1590" — the initials of Lady Ursula Walsingham, who took over the tenancy of the local Manor round about this date. She was the widow of Sir Francis Walsingham, Secretary of State to Queen Elizabeth I.

Bearing away to the right (NE) on leaving the tithe barn, you soon come to a lane which takes you the final few yards into Sydling village — a delightful place situated along the banks of a crystal clear stream called Sydling Water.

The village has a pleasant pub, "The Greyhound Inn", and here, if you have timed your arrival sensibly, you can pause for refreshment before starting the next stage of the walk. Retracing your steps down Sydling's main street, you turn left into East Street. Near the end of this street a fingerpost, pointing to the right, reads: "Bridleway to Large Bar Barn". Your route lies along this lane, and soon it swings E and begins climbing a steep hill. When, after about ¼ mile, the lane makes a sharp right-hand turn, you leave the beaten track and continue straight on (E) through a gateway.

This takes you into a grassy field, with clear traces of a turf covered bridleway leading uphill towards another gate about 200 yards distant. After passing through this second gate you soon come to a fork in the path. Take the right-hand fork, which runs almost due E alongside a hedge. After passing through two more gates you leave the guiding hedge behind, and head ENE up an open grassy hillside. Soon you'll arrive on the crest of a ridge, where an ancient turf track runs alongside a hedge.

Turn right (SSE) along this ridgeway, passing close to the summit of Large Bar Hill (735 ft) and through a series of gates.

After half a mile you'll see an area of thick woodland a little way down the hillside on your right. This is known as The Poorlots, and back in the 1940's an old shepherd told me that in his grandfather's day the poor people of Nether Cerne (a once-flourishing village which has now become depopulated) used to trudge up here from the valley below to gather firewood. The paths they used to follow over Ridge Hill have now disappeared under the plough, but traces of them still exist in the shape of two small gateways in the hedgerow on your left.

Continuing along the ridgeway, look out for a spot where the hedge and fence on your left makes a sudden right-angled bend to the E. Just around the corner of this bend you'll see a small *wooden* bridleway gate set in the hedge. DON'T pass through this gate; instead, continue E along the hedge for a few more yards until you come to a small *metal* bridleway gate. Pass through this into a small grassy field, and continue E through another bridleway gate only a few yards away.

You now find yourself in a large arable field with a hedge on your left running due E. However, the 1:25000 map shows the bridleway running along the other side of the hedge, and just beyond this last gate you'll see a place where you can cross into the next field.

You now continue due E, keeping as close as possible to the hedgerow to avoid damaging the crop. Eventually, after passing through two more gates, and keeping the hedge on your right-hand all the way, you arrive on the A352 Godmanstone — Cerne Abbas road.

Almost immediately opposite you, on the other side of the road, you'll see a little-used green lane running downhill to the banks of the tiny River Cerne. Here a footbridge enables you to cross to the far bank, where a pleasant grassy footpath runs alongside the stream in both directions.

Turn right (S) after crossing the bridge. Keeping close company with the stream, you soon find yourself approaching Godmanstone village. It is easy to pick out the tiny thatched roof of the "Smith's Arms' on the far side of the stream, and a few yards farther on you come to a footbridge which takes you across the river to the village street and your parked car.

Points of Interest

Sydling St. Nicholas Church stands in a picturesque setting, half-hidden among trees. Parts of the building date from the 15th Century, including the tower (1430) and the north porch (1480). One unusual feature of this porch is a fireplace — a relic of the days when the porch was the meeting place for the parish council!

The font is of particular interest, as it is reputed to have been fashioned from the capital of an early Roman pillar. This rather crude "conversion job" was certainly carried out over 1000 years ago, and possibly as far back as pre-Saxon days.

Another noteworthy item is the rather battered early 13th Century oak chest with a coin slot in its lid. It is furnished with three locks — presumably so that the vicar and two churchwardens could each hold a key.

The church clock has been tolling out the hours to the villagers since 1593. Its mechanism combines simplicity with sturdiness, and tradition has it that it was made by a local blacksmith. If this is true then he was no mean craftsman, because this is one of the oldest clocks still working in England. Incidentally, it has no external dial, being designed simply to strike the hours.

Sydling Court. This venerable manor house is situated close alongside the church, but is almost hidden by a thick screen of trees. Many famous people over the centuries have lived here and presided over the affairs of the village. Besides Sir Francis Walsingham, mentioned previously, and his widow, Lady Ursula, there was Sir Philip Sidney, another notable Elizabethan. It was Sir Philip who, when mortally wounded in the siege of Zutphen, ignored his own craving for a drink and passed his water bottle to a dying soldier with the immortal words: "Thy necessity is yet greater than mine".

Wayside Cross. At the foot of Church Lane, where it joins Sydling's village street, you will see the remains of a wayside cross of golden-hued stone. It dates from early medieval times. The upper part of the cross has long since disappeared, and all that now remains is an octagonal base, and the lower part of an octagonal shaft.

Walk No. 13

The Gibraltar of Wessex

A circular walk around Portland Bill.
Distance: Approx. 4 miles.
O.S. Map: Explorer OL15 (1:25000); or 194 (1:50000).

SOMETIMES referred to as "the Gibraltar of Wessex", the rocky and windswept Portland peninsula juts out 4½ miles into the English Channel. It is a place of strange contrasts where medieval strip fields lie cheek by jowl with a large harbour, modern dock facilities and a strategically situated Coastguard helicopter station. Where small towns of grey stone cottages rise tier upon tier up steep hillsides, or appear to teeter precariously on the brink of deep stone quarries.

Exposed to three points of the compass, Portland's craggy coastline looks out over one of the most dangerous tide-races in Europe. However, this does not deter the local fishermen who (sea conditions permitting) casually launch their small open boats over the edge of vertical cliffs by means of primitive hand-operated cranes fashioned from massive baulks of timber.

To sum up, anyone who has an eye for the unusual will find this rocky outpost of Dorset a strangely fascinating place.

To reach the starting point of this walk you drive across the road bridge on to Portland, and then head up the steep, winding hill through Fortuneswell on to the Portland Heights. Here, near a prominent obelisk-shaped memorial, I suggest you park the car for a few minutes to admire the magnificent view of the 18 miles long Chesil Beach. If the day is clear you will also see the beautiful sun-glowing headland of Golden Cap. (See companion booklet, *West Dorset Walks*).

Returning to the car, you continue along the road signposted "Portland Bill" until, about ¾-mile beyond the Pennsylvania Castle Hotel, you will see a "Public Footpath" fingerpost pointing down an unsurfaced lane leading off to the left. Drive down this lane for about 100 yards and park in a large lay-by.

Commence your walk by heading downhill to the cliff-edge overlooking Freshwater Bay; then turn right (S) and follow the cliff-edge track which leads towards Portland Bill. There is nearly always plenty to hold one's interest along this stretch, with naval and commercial vessels going about their business, and possibly a cluster of bass fishing boats on the fringe of the foam-flecked tide-race.

Soon the path leads you past Cave Hole — a wave-gulping cavern with a "blow-hole" in its roof. In stormy weather this hole belches forth columns of spray and wind-driven spindrift.

After rounding Portland Bill, with its lighthouse, refreshment kiosks and famous Pulpit Rock, you skirt the perimeter fence of a Ministry of Defence establishment until, just outside the entrance gate, you'll see a grassy path heading NW towards the cliffs again. Continue past the Coastguard Lookout, and around the grassy rim of Wallsend Cove — a favourite hunting ground of wind-hovering kestrels.

About 300 yards after passing another big M.O.D. complex, you'll come to a farm track which heads inland (ESE) past some ancient stripfields. Turn down this track, which will soon bring you out on to a tarred road. Follow this for about ½-mile, maintaining an E direction whenever you come to a road junction. This will bring you to the "Eight Kings" public house in Southwell. Turn right at the pub; then take the first left turning down a rough quarry road. From the right-hand side of this road you can look directly down into the stone quarry, which is still operating.

Continue down this road to the cliff-edge, where you turn left. You are now back on the track you set out along on the early stages of this walk, and very soon you arrive back at the parked car.

Points of Interest

Portland Museum. This small museum, containing exhibits of local interest, is housed in a typical old (1640) Portland stone cottage. Alongside the cottage is a path leading down to Church Ope Cove and Rufus Castle. Before commencing its final steep descent to the beach, the path passes beneath the ruins of Rufus Castle, reputed to have been built by William Rufus, son of the Conqueror. The castle's craggy situation and 7 ft thick walls appear well-nigh impregnable, but in 1142 it was besieged and captured by Robert of Gloucester, illegitimate son of Henry I, while fighting on behalf of his sister Matilda during her attempt to dethrone Stephen.

Just above the beach is the graveyard and all that remains of the old parish church of Portland, destroyed long ago by a landslip.

Walk No. 14

The Magic of White Nothe

Osmington Mills — Ringstead — Burning Cliff — White
Nothe — Falcon Barn — South Down Farm — Ringstead
Medieval Village — Osmington Mills
Distance: Approx. 8 miles
O.S. Map: Explorer OL15 (1:25000); or 194 (1:50000).

THE longshore fishing hamlet of Osmington Mills
lies in a secluded little valley, some 5 miles east of
Weymouth. A small stream flows past the cottages before
finding its way into the sea through a narrow gap in the
cliffs. There is a car park overlooking the bay, and a pub
(The Smugglers Inn) which serves meals and snacks.

After parking your car you head E along the coast
path which, rather surprisingly, begins by leading you
down some steps almost to the bar door of the Smugglers
Inn. Turning left, you skirt around the pub and continue
past a row of old tar-coated coastguard cottages. After
crossing a stile you head upwards across a grassy field to

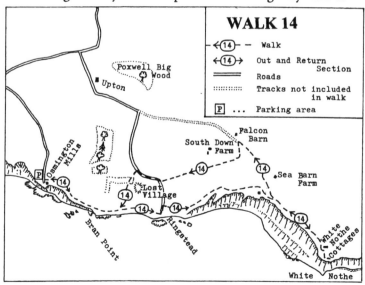

the nearby cliff edge, and from there onwards the coast path is clearly waymarked.

Beneath the cliff, if the tide is out, you will see the waves breaking over numerous flat rocks which bear such names as Hannah's Ledge, Frenchman's Ledge, Pool Ledge and Bran Ledge. These rocks, hidden at high water, have been the undoing of many a storm-driven vessel, and the stark ribs of one victim will be seen jutting up out of the water as you walk along towards Bran Point.

On breasting the low hill above this small promontory there opens up before you a magnificent view of cliff-encircled Ringstead Bay, with the spectacular chalk-white buttresses of White Nothe headland dominating everything. Soon you come to a small wooded coombe, which the path crosses by two flights of steps.

A ¼-mile beyond this lies Ringstead's cluster of modern seaside bungalows. After these have been left behind the coast path soon begins to climb through blackthorn thickets, and around the upper edge of a longshore landslip known as "Burning Cliff". The name originated in 1826, when chemical reactions in the rocks created heat which ignited the oil-rich clays.

After skirting the grounds of Holworth House you begin the final stretch to the summit of White Nothe, where a row of old coastguard cottages overlook the nearby cliff edge. To obtain the best view from this vantage point you should walk S from the cottages towards a derelict wartime lookout post near the cliff edge, and then turn left and continue along a grassy path for about 70 yards. You will be rewarded with an unforgettable view of Bat's Head and the natural rock arch at the base of its vertical dazzling white cliffs. WARNING: Do not venture too close to the cliff edge because the steeply sloping grass becomes very slippery when damp.

You begin the return route by retracing your steps along the cliff path for about ¾-mile, but instead of making the final steep descent to Holworth House you bear away NW across the turf, passing lonely Sea Barn Farm on its W side.

About 200 yards NW of this building you come to a lane and some National Trust information boards. Nearby you will see a gated track (classified as a bridleway) leading off to the NW. Follow this track for ¼-mile until you come to a fingerpost pointing off to your left (S) which reads: "Ringstead Beach ¾-mile". Take the blackthorn-flanked path it indicates until you come to a stile. Immediately after crossing this stile you will see a side path heading off to your right (SW). This soon brings you out into a grassy field, with South Down Farmhouse about ¼-mile distant. A right of way, with no visible path, heads WSW across the fields, passing through a gate just S of the farm buildings. It then continues WSW along the steadily descending crest of a grassy ridge, until eventually it brings you to a footbridge and a stile. You then continue to a second stile only a few yards further on, and this brings you out on to a narrow tarred lane.

Follow this lane in a WNW direction for ¼-mile until, shortly after passing a bungalow and a small spinney on your left, you see an unsurfaced lane branching off to the left. Although marked "Private Road" it is a pedestrian right of way, and you follow it for about 100 yards until it splits into three tracks. Take the middle track (see NOTE below) which soon leads you into a grassy field that is full of intriguing mounds and hollows.

These turf-covered mounds conceal all that remains of the ancient village of Ringstead. Mentioned in the Domesday Book, it remained a thriving little community of farming and fisherfolk until, so local tradition tells us, it was destroyed by pirates.

Standing in this secluded field, it is difficult to imagine the scene on that fateful day, long ago, when the life of a peaceful village ended with the screams of terrified women and children, and the crackling roar of burning thatch.

Heading across the top NW corner of the field, you

come to a public footpath which runs down through a wooded coombe towards the nearby beach. This is the path used by those long-departed villagers to reach their fishing boats, and it is interesting to see that a few locals still use it today for the same purpose.

The path soon brings you back to the double flight of steps that you encountered on the outward leg of your walk, and from this point you return to Osmington Mills by retracing your steps along the cliff path.

NOTE: In wet weather it may be preferable to take the right-hand track, and then bear left along a disused military road which skirts the edge of the "ruined village" field. This, too, leads back to the double flight of steps near the mouth of the wooded coombe.

Walk No. 15

Lulworth Cove to Bat's Head

Lulworth Cove — Durdle Door — Bat's Head — Scratchy Bottom — Durdle Door — St. Oswald's Bay (low tide only) — Lulworth Cove

Distances: Complete walk approx. 5¼ miles; shortened walk to Durdle Door only — 2½ miles.

O.S. Map: Explorer OL15 (1:25000); or 194 (1:50000).

LULWORTH COVE was created many thousands of years ago after sea erosion opened up a weak joint in the hard Portland limestone which, at that time, formed the outer wall of the cliffs. This allowed the pounding waves to wear away the softer rocks and clays immediately behind the cliffs, forming a deep hollow among the coastal hills. The final result, as we see it today, is an oyster-shaped cove of quite exceptional beauty, where small fishing craft and cruising yachts find sheltered anchorage.

It must be said, however, that Lulworth Cove becomes rather crowded during the peak holiday months,

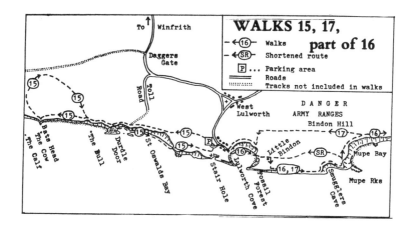

and to see this beauty spot at its best one should preferably visit it in early spring or late autumn — or, perhaps best of all, on a crisp sunny day in winter. The walk described here is particularly suitable for winter because the cliff paths are well drained and comparatively free of mud.

You begin by following the clearly defined white track which heads W from Lulworth Cove car park, climbing around the steep grassy flank of Hambury Tout, and then along the cliff-top until you see Durdle Door beach below. A path with roughly fashioned steps descends to this beautiful swimming and picnic spot, which owes its name to a large natural rock arch that is shaped like a Gothic doorway.

Incidentally, if you decide to break your walk at Durdle Door for a swim, do not venture out too far as there are strong tidal currents beyond the rocky promontory.

From Durdle Door you continue W along the cliff-top path (NOT along the beach), descending before long into the mouth of a deep coombe called Scratchy Bottom (!). Pause here for a moment to note the position of three stiles at the lower end of a strip of arable land in the valley bottom. You will be crossing these stiles on your return journey.

Meanwhile you continue along the coast path, which at this point makes its way up a very steep grassy slope. When you pause for breath near the top, be sure to look back over your shoulder — the view is magnificent, and extends to distant St. Aldhelm's Head.

Ahead of you the seascape is dominated by the precipitous white cliffs of Bat's Head. Through the base of this unusual promontory the pounding waves have driven a rock arch, whilst alongside it a spectacular rock stack emerges from the inshore shallows.

Upon reaching the summit of Bat's Head you cross a stile a few yards behind the cliff-top. This gives access on to an area of rough hillside grassland called the Warren, with a steep-sided coombe falling away on your right-hand side. Head NW and then N around the rim of this coombe. This will take you steadily up the hillside, and after you have walked inland for about ¼-mile you veer NE and then E, following a right-of-way which skirts the steep inland end of the coombe. There is no visible path, but if you keep to the reasonably level ground alongside the rim of the coombe you cannot go far wrong.

Eventually you will come to a wire boundary fence. Turn right (S) along this and very soon you'll come to a stile. Cross this, and then descend in a SE direction down the side of the next coombe. This is Scratchy Bottom, which you passed on the outward leg of your journey. Cross the three stiles at the lower end of the valley, and make your way back along the cliff-top path to Durdle Door.

If you have timed this part of the walk to coincide with low tide, you can now return to Lulworth Cove by walking E along the beach to the far end of St. Oswald's Bay, and then up through a gap in the cliffs and along a public footpath which emerges on to a tarred lane. Turn left down this lane and it will very soon bring you back to the car park.

Points of Interest

Stair Hole. This spectacular example of sea erosion, with its wave-gulping rock arches, can be viewed only 100 yards S of Lulworth Cove car park. It is particularly interesting because it demonstrates a similar erosion process to the one which long ago created Lulworth Cove. Notice, too, how the exposed rock strata, originally laid down in horizontal beds, have been tilted and folded. This upheaval took place during a period of huge earth movements which also saw the formation of the Alps.

Walk No. 16

Lulworth Cove to Kimmeridge Bay

Lulworth Cove car park - Kimmeridge Bay car park
Distance: Approx. 8 miles.
O.S. Map: Explorer OL15 (1:25000); or 194 (1:50000).

WARNING

FROM a point just E of Lulworth Cove, as far as the W side of Kimmeridge Bay, some 7000 acres of land are used for Army gunnery ranges. However, a number of coastal and inland footpaths, clearly defined by yellow-banded waymark posts at 50-100 yards intervals, have been cleared of explosives and are open to the public ON THOSE DAYS WHEN THE RANGES ARE NOT IN USE. At the time of writing these "open" days occur on all but six weekends a year, during public holidays (including a two-week period around Christmas), and throughout August. For up-to-date information 'phone (01929) 462721.

* * * * *

A SPECTACULARLY beautiful cliff path follows the coastline for the whole extent of the Army gunnery ranges, from Lulworth Cove to Kimmeridge Bay. Access by the public is limited to the periods detailed in the WARNING above.

Many experienced ramblers consider this to be the most beautiful stretch of coast in Dorset, and although very hilly in places it is certainly well worth the effort. Alternatively, it is possible to explore the same magnificent stretch of coastline by means of the circular walks Nos. 17 and 18.

Walk No. 17

A Fossil Forest and a Smuggler's Cave

Lulworth Cove — Little Bindon — Fossil Forest — Mupe
Bay — Bindon Hill — Radar Hill — Lulworth Cove
Distance: Approx. 5 miles; shortened version — 4 miles.
O.S. Map: Explorer OL15 (1:25000); or 194 (1:50000).

IMPORTANT — This walk is over Ministry of Defence
land, and public access is limited to certain dates and
waymarked footpaths. See WARNING under Walk No.
16.

FROM the car park at Lulworth Cove make your
way down to the shore; then walk along the beach to the
NE corner of the cove. Here, near a gap in the cliffs, a
fingerpost indicates a footpath leading to: "Coast Path
and Range Walks". Follow this path until, near the
remains of a 13th century chapel (see under *Points of
Interest*), you pass through a gate on to the Army ranges.
Here you turn right towards the nearby cliff-edge, where
steps lead down to the fossilised remains of a forest which
flourished 120 million years ago. The actual trees are no
longer visible, but you can still see the fossilized growths
of algae which once surrounded the trunks.

Continuing E along the cliff-top path, you soon find
yourself looking down into a rocky, cliff-encircled cove
known as Bacon Hole. At the W end of this cove, near the
base of the cliffs, there is a genuine smugglers' cave. Until
well into early 1800's it was used by the Lulworth
fishermen as a hiding place for kegs of contraband spirits.

A few yards farther on, around the next
promontory, lies Mupe Bay. Steps lead down the cliffs to
this delightful beach of mixed shingle and gritty sand.
Sheltered from the main force of the tides and prevailing
W winds, it is a pleasant spot to pause for a swim.

On the cliff-top immediately above Mupe Bay is a
fingerpost. One arm points W, and reads: "To Little
Bindon". This is the return route for those opting for the

shortened version of this walk. However, if you have the time and energy, I strongly recommend you to continue NE up the steep grassy flank of Bindon Hill.

On reaching the summit you will be rewarded with a magnificent view of the vast Dorset heathlands, stretching all the way to the shores of Poole Harbour and beyond.

A spectacular ridgeway runs W along the crest of Bindon Hill, and another fingerpost indicates your return route along it to Lulworth Cove by way of Radar Hill. Shortly after passing the radar installations that have given the hill its name, you emerge from the Army ranges by another gate.

Just outside this gate you turn left and follow a footpath leading down to a stile. After crossing this stile you turn right on to another path which skirts the cliff-edge overlooking Lulworth Cove. On approaching the W end of the cove it descends steeply to the road leading back through the village to the car park.

Points of Interest

Little Bindon. Around 1150 the Cistercian abbey of Bindon was founded on the high ground overlooking the E side of Lulworth Cove. It is possible the monks found this spot too bleak and windswept, because in 1172 they moved inland to Wool where a "new" Bindon Abbey flourished for many centuries.

However, in the 13th century a small chapel was built above Lulworth Cove close to the site of the original abbey.

It is unusual in having a small cottage attached to its W end. The chapel, with its arched windows blocked up, is no longer used for services, but at the time of writing the adjoining cottage appears to be still inhabited.

Walk No. 18

A Ghost Village and a Phantom Army

Tyneham — Worbarrow Tout — Flower's Barrow —
Whiteway Hill — Tyneham
Distance: Approx. 4 miles
O.S. Map: Explorer OL15 (1:25000); or 194 (1:50000).

IN 1943, when the Second World War was
approaching its climax, the War Office decided to turn
the countryside around the picturesque little Doomsday
village of Tyneham into a gunnery range. So the 225
people living in the parish were evacuated from their 102
dwellings, with the promise that they would be allowed
to return after the war was over.

Unfortunately for those dispossessed villagers, the
promise was never kept. Their native place remains
forbidden territory, except for limited "open" periods
when the public is allowed access to the beautiful little
village church and to some spectacular waymarked

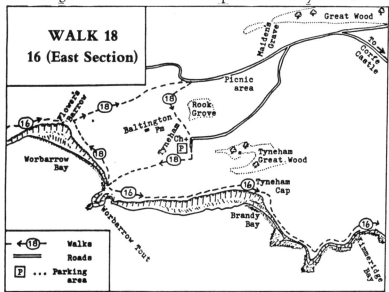

WALK 18
16 (East Section)

footpaths. (See WARNING, Walk No. 16). On these open days one can drive a car to Tyneham and park it on the outskirts of the village.

Tyneham church contains an exhibition which provides a fascinating insight into the lives of the departed villagers. I suggest you visit this first of all, because it will add considerably to the interest of your walk. Also, of course, it is best to enter the church before getting your boots muddy!

From the car park a track leads you down a pleasant valley to the longshore beacon hill called Worbarrow Tout. This distinctive promontory is flanked on either side by beaches which are accessible to the public when the range walks are open.

From Worbarrow Tout you cross the mouth of a small stream and head up the steep cliff path to the summit of the Iron Age hill fort of Flower's Barrow. Your reward at the end of this climb will be an extensive gull's-eye view of the neighbouring coast and countryside, with Lulworth Castle flanked by woodlands away to the NW.

It is probable that the early Celtic inhabitants of Flower's Barrow were attacked and defeated by the same Roman army that later overwhelmed the defences of Maiden Castle. (See Walk No. 7). Local tradition has it that the ghostly image of that Roman army still appears from time to time on the ancient hill tracks around Flower's Barrow. The first recorded sighting was in 1678, when over a hundred local inhabitants witnessed the phantom legion on its route march through eternity. Over the years there have been many similar sightings, including several in the 20th century.

From Flower's Barrow a prehistoric ridgeway path heads inland in a NE direction, crossing the summit of Whiteway Hill (607 ft) before approaching the Corfe — Lulworth road. Here, about ½-mile W of the Maiden's Grave (see under *Points of Interest*), you turn right on to a signposted track which leads downhill to Tyneham village and your parked car.

Points of Interest

Tyneham's history stretches back a long way, and in the 11th century the manor was held by Robert de Mortain, half-brother to William the Conqueror. The once-beautiful old manor house was evacuated in 1943 by Ralph Bond, the last squire of Tyneham. His family had lived in the house since 1583, and its ruination from neglect and vandalism, and the knowledge that he would never return, caused him great anguish. He died in 1952, and in 1968 the main Elizabethan section of the house was demolished by the authorities, leaving the 14th century hall at the rear, with its great oak beams and trusses, to moulder and crumble slowly into decay.

Maiden's Grave and the Coffin Tree. As you walk NE along the ridgeway track from Flower's Barrow you will see the ruins of Baltington Farm below the hillside on your right. Many years ago a young girl hanged herself in the cowshed of the farm. In those days a suicide could not be given a Christian burial in a churchyard, so the unfortunate girl was buried on the parish boundary, where it runs alongside the Corfe — Lulworth road. The spot is still referred to as the Maiden's Grave, and an ancient oak which stands nearby is known as the Coffin Tree because on its bark some unknown hands long ago carved a memorial to the girl in the shape of a small coffin.

Walk No. 19

Exploring St Aldhelm's Head

Worth Matravers — St Aldhelm's Head — Winspit —
Seacombe Quarry — Dancing Ledge — Priest's Way —
Worth Matravers
Distances: (i) Full circuit via Dancing Ledge — 9 miles;
(ii) return via Seacombe Bottom - 6¼ miles; (iii) return
via Winspit Bottom — 5¼ miles.
O.S. Map: Explorer OL15 (1:25000); or 195 (1:50000).

THIS very interesting walk includes several miles of
spectacular coastline, and is a "must" for anyone
exploring this part of southern Purbeck. It begins in the
ancient village of Worth Matravers, with its picturesque
stone cottages, duckpond and pub, "The Square and
Compass".

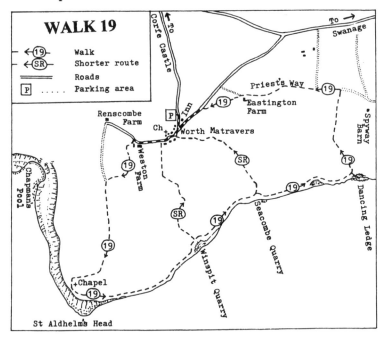

There is a public car park just a few yards up the road from the pub. From here you walk downhill into the village, where the ancient church is well worth a visit. (See under *Points of Interest*).

From the church you take the road leading W out of the village. After passing some farm buildings and a tall green silo tower you turn left (SW) on to a lane (classified as a public footpath) which is bordered by a sign saying: "Private Road — Weston Farm and Coastguard Cottages". From here you follow a clearly waymarked route to St Aldhelm's Head — or St Alban's Head as it is often called. The Ordnance Survey map plays safe by quoting both names, but the small Norman chapel on top of the headland is dedicated to St Aldhelm who, in 705, became the first bishop of Sherborne.

The chapel was built between 1150 and 1200, and its interior combines stark simplicity with a most interesting vaulted roof which rests upon a massive central column. Over the centuries the masonry of this column has become covered with the initials of many former men of Worth. Studying these inscriptions, I was puzzled by the fact that a disproportionate number bore the date 1665 — until my wife reminded me that in this year the Great Plague was decimating the population of England. Faced with the prospect of a horrible death, and burial in a mass grave, perhaps the folk who carved their names and initials in the chapel were seeking to leave at least some evidence of their brief existence on this planet.

Heading E past the Coastguard Lookout, you follow the cliff-path around the mouth of the beautiful Winspit valley, which is flanked by two turf-covered hills called West Man and East Man. Both hills are terraced with strip lynchets — the result of contour ploughing with oxen under the medieval open field system.

These hills have also been mined for their high quality stone, and the abandoned cave quarries overlooking the sea extend for up to 200 feet into the hillside. They are a favourite roosting place for bats, and naturalists have recorded seventeen different species in the Winspit workings.

Continuing along the coast path, you soon descend into the mouth of another valley known as Seacombe Bottom. Here, too, there has been extensive underground quarrying, and the caves were used to conceal many a contraband cargo in the days when smuggling was part of the way of life along this coast. A grass-grown track, once used by those smugglers and quarry workers, meanders up the deep and lonely valley to Worth Matravers, making a round trip of about 6¼ miles.

However, if you still have the time and energy, I strongly recommend you to continue E along the coast path for another mile. This will bring you to an outjutting rock platform known as Dancing Ledge — so-called because at certain states of the tides the waves surge over the rock with an erratic "dancing" motion.

Above the Ledge, alongside two adjoining stiles, you will see a waymark stone with arrows indicating the routes to Langton (1¼ miles) and Spyway Barn (¾ mile). Take the Langton path, which climbs in a NW direction up the grassy hillside. At the top you will come to another waymark stone. Here you bear left over a stile. (DO NOT follow the arrow pointing to Langton). Immediately after crossing the stile turn right (N) along a track which soon takes you alongside a working quarry and then brings you out on to an ancient packhorse trail known as the Priest's Way.

Turn left (W) and follow the Priest's Way for about a mile until you come to a stone stile near Eastington Farm. Here a fingerpost indicates a choice of two routes back to Worth Matravers. One (bearing WNW) is the final grassed-over stretch of the Priest's Way, and the other (bearing WSW) is a grassy field path. I would recommend the latter because it skirts the top end of the Seacombe valley, offering a magnificent view through this beautifully contoured cleft in the hills.

This path takes you to the outskirts of the village. Turn left on reaching the tarred road, and soon you'll arrive back at your parked car.

Points of Interest

Worth Matravers Church contains many interesting features. Dedicated to St Nicholas of Myra, it was built, with later additions, around 1100 on the site of an earlier Saxon church. The beautiful chancel arch enriched with chevron moulding, is a particularly fine piece of craftsmanship.

In the churchyard, near the N side of the church, is the grave of Benjamin Jesty, a local farmer who successfully inoculated his family against smallpox many years before this medical breakthrough was "discovered" by Dr Edward Jenner. His epitaph tells us that he died in 1810, aged 79 years. Also that he was "the first person known that introduced Cow Pox by inoculation and who from his great strength of mind made the Experiment from the Cow on his wife and two Sons".

One is left with the uneasy feeling that he might have displayed even more "strength of mind" if he had first made the experiment on himself!

In the church porch you will also notice a slab of carved Purbeck marble, shaped like a coffin lid. This was ploughed up in 1957 about ¼-mile NNE of St Aldhelm's Chapel, and has been dated 1250–1275. Beneath it was found a grave containing a female skeleton, and close by were the foundations and wall rubble of a small square stone building which may have been the "cell" of an anchoress (female hermit).

The Priest's Way. This ancient trackway links Worth Matravers with Swanage. Centuries ago, when Swanage was just a small longshore village, the priest from Worth used to trudge along this track to hold services for the isolated community of fisherfolk. The route he travelled is still known as "The Priest's Way".

Shipwrecks have occurred along this rockbound stretch of coast since time immemorial, but one of the worst disasters was the loss of the East Indiaman, *Halsewell,* in January 1786 with the loss of 168 lives, including those of the captain, two of his daughters and five other young ladies. The vessel was pounded to pieces on the rocks between Winspit and Seacombe, but amazingly 82 survivors managed to cling to a sloping wave-pounded rock, and from there were hauled to safety on ropes lowered by local quarrymen, at considerable risk to their own lives.

Incidentally, amongst the piles of splintered driftwood washed up after the disaster there was found a decorated mirror from the wreck. Amazingly, it was quite undamaged. Today in hangs in the church at Worth Matravers. You will find it over the arch of the main door.

===

Walk No. 20

From Swanage to Dancing Ledge

Durlston Country Park — Tilly Whim Caves — Anvil
Point — Dancing Ledge — Upper Coast Path — Durlston
Country Park
Distance: Approx. 6½ miles.
O.S. Map: Explorer OL15 (1:25000); or 194 (1:50000).

START from the public car park in the Durlston
Country Park — a popular beauty spot situated only 1
mile from the centre of Swanage. Take the signposted
path which heads downhill to the famous Great Globe of
the World, carved from eight huge interlocking sections
of Portland stone weighing some 40 tons.

Continuing SW along the cliff path, you soon pass
the entrance to some old quarry workings called the Tilly
Whim Caves. Like most longshore cliff quarries along this

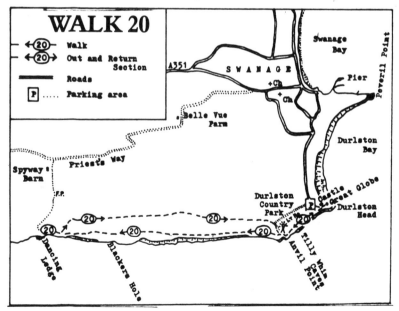

coast, these underground workings were once used by smugglers as a hiding place for contraband goods.

The coast path now takes you past Anvil Point Lighthouse, and then along a lonely and beautiful cliff-top track. The stretch of path about ½-mile either side of the National Trust "Belle Vue" sign is used by badgers on their nocturnal hunting forays, so look out for their distinctive broad paw prints if the path happens to be muddy.

In due course the path descends to Dancing Ledge — a wave-washed rock platform backed by more underground stone quarries. On leaving Dancing Ledge, retrace your steps eastwards for ¼-mile along the cliff path until you come to a waymark pointing off to your left (NE) which reads: "Upper Path to Durlston". Follow this path up a steep hillside until, on reaching the crest of the slope, it veers almost due E and levels out. The views from this upper path are magnificent, and extend from St Aldhelm's Head to the Isle of Wight.

On re-entering Durlston Country Park, the path crosses the grass-grown hillocks of some long-abandoned stone quarries, and then descends to Anvil Point Lighthouse. From here you retrace your original route back to the parked car.